Changes to Ear

by Marcia K.

PEARSON
Scott
Foresman

How does Earth's surface wear away?

Earth's Crust

Earth is covered by a rock layer called the crust. The crust is underwater in the ocean.

Earth's crust has many natural features. Each one is called a **landform.** Landforms are many sizes and shapes. Plains are flat landforms on low ground. Plateaus are flat landforms on high ground. Peninsulas are landforms that stick out into water. Valleys and canyons are also landforms.

Some landforms develop quickly. Others take a long time. A mountain may take millions of years to form. Rocks rolling downward can change it quickly. Think of how a flood moves soil from one place to another. Think about dust that blows across empty, unplanted fields.

How Weathering Affects Landforms

Landforms are always changing. Rocks slowly break into smaller pieces. This process is called **weathering.** Water, ice, and temperature changes can cause weathering. Chemicals and living things cause weathering too.

Physical Weathering

In physical weathering, rock breaks into smaller pieces of the same kind of rock. Water can cause physical weathering. Flowing water carries small bits of soil and sand. These bits scrape against rocks to wear them down.

Ice also causes physical weathering. Rain or melting snow can get into cracks in rocks. If this water freezes, it turns into ice. The ice pushes against the cracks. The cracks become deeper. This process can repeat until the rock finally splits.

Changes in temperature can also weather rocks. A rock's surface grows larger when it gets hot. Its surface shrinks when it gets cold. All this changing may weaken the rock.

Living things can also cause weathering. Have you seen plants living in the cracks of rocks? As plants and roots grow, they can split the rocks.

Weathering changed the rock known as the Old Man of the Mountain in New Hampshire. In 2003 the rock broke off and fell.

Chemical Weathering

In chemical weathering, rock breaks into smaller pieces. But the material that the rock is made of also changes.

Different materials can be formed when chemicals come in contact with rock. Carbon dioxide, a chemical in the air, mixes with rainwater and forms a weak acid. When it rains, this acid lands on the rock. It combines with rock material and forms a new chemical. Over time, the new chemical breaks the rock into smaller pieces.

Chemicals can come from animals and plants. These chemicals can cause weathering. So can people and their activities.

As water moves, it weathers rock and carries it to new places.

5

How do weathered materials move?

Effects of Erosion

Erosion is the process of moving weathered rock. Water, ice, gravity, and wind can cause erosion.

Rain can wash away loose rock material into a stream. The stream may carry that material far away.

Over time, water running downhill carves grooves into the land. These grooves become canyons or valleys.

Waves pound against cracks in rocks that are at the shore. Pieces of rock break off and are carried away. As the shore erodes, new landforms, such as beaches, will appear.

Millions of years ago, huge ice sheets, called glaciers, covered parts of Earth. A glacier slowly slides along a thin layer of water below it, wearing away rock. Even small glaciers can rip rocks apart and carry the pieces far away.

Deposition

Wind and water carry bits of rock and soil from one place to another. **Deposition** is the laying down of pieces of Earth's surface. This may happen slowly or very quickly.

When water moves slowly, big pebbles in the water sink first. Then smaller bits, such as sand, sink. Finally the smallest pieces of soil, called silt, fall to the bottom. Rivers deposit material where they meet the ocean. This deposit forms a fan-shaped landform called a delta.

Wind can carry only small bits of rock. In deserts, the wind deposits sand in mounds called sand dunes. Wind will keep shaping the dunes.

Gravity and Landslides

No place on Earth is completely flat. The force of gravity pulls all objects from high places to lower ones. Gravity causes loose material to roll downhill. Bits of rock and soil may move slowly, only a little at a time. But at times they move very quickly. Heavy rains or earthquakes can loosen material that is on a steep hill or slope. Gravity then pulls this loose material downward. A **landslide** is the quick downhill movement of great amounts of rock and soil. Buildings, trees, and other large objects may be swept down the slope with the sliding soil.

Gravity and Avalanches

The rapid movement of objects down a slope can occur in cold areas as well. An avalanche is fast-moving snow and ice that race down a mountain. Strong winds, earthquakes, and explosions can cause avalanches. People try to stop avalanches from happening. They may clear snow before it builds up too much. Landslides and avalanches can cause terrible damage, especially on large mountains.

Controlling Erosion and Deposition

Erosion and deposition often take place in areas with few trees or plants. Trees and plants help keep wind and water from eroding rock and soil.

People have found ways to slow the effects of erosion. They grow plants on the sides of hills. Roots hold soil in place. Plant leaves keep some of the rain from washing soil away. Farmers whose fields are on a hill can plow them into steps, called terraces. Rain forms puddles on the steps instead of washing soil downhill. Crops can then soak up more water.

Erosion can be a problem along the seashore as well. Waves that pound against the shore carry away material, such as sand. People build barriers to prevent this. Barriers stop waves from eroding sand and rock. Barriers also help protect nearby buildings and roads.

People can reduce deposition. They can dig away deposits from waterways. This helps ships pass through the water more easily.

Terraces slow the movement of water running downhill.

How can Earth's surface change rapidly?

Volcanoes

A volcano is a landform. It can cause a rapid change to Earth's surface. Hot rock, called magma, has partly melted into liquid. Gases push the magma up. A **volcano** forms at a weak spot in Earth's crust.

A volcano erupts when magma reaches the surface. Lava is magma that has come out of a volcano. Lava is still red hot.

Pressure can build so much that the gases in the magma explode. Lava, gases, and ashes burst out of openings called vents. Not all volcanoes erupt so wildly. Magma oozes up and slowly flows out of some volcanoes. A bowl-shaped area, or crater, may form around the volcano's main opening.

The 1980 eruption of Mount St. Helens sent rock and ash into the air.

Effects of Eruptions

When volcanoes erupt, they form ash and new rock. Ash from the eruption of Mount St. Helens in 1980 flew more than 24 kilometers (15 miles) into the air. It covered nearby cities. It killed trees and animals.

Active and Dormant Volcanoes

An active volcano erupts often or shows signs that it will erupt. Kilauea in Hawaii began its latest eruption in 1983. It is still actively erupting.

A dormant volcano has not erupted for a long time. Mount Rainier in Washington has not had a big eruption in more than 500 years. If it erupted, it could melt nearby glaciers. This could cause flooding and landslides.

An extinct volcano no longer erupts. Mount Kenya in Africa is one of many extinct volcanoes in the world.

Earth's Moving Plates

Earth's crust rests on a layer called the upper mantle. These layers form huge moving pieces called plates.

The Cause of Earthquakes

A **fault** is a break or crack in rocks where Earth's crust can move. Rocks may get stuck along a fault. The plates keep moving. They press on the rocks that are stuck. If the pressure becomes strong enough, the rocks break. The plates shift quickly. An **earthquake** is the sudden movement that makes Earth's crust shake.

The focus is the underground spot where the plates shift and the earthquake begins. The **epicenter** is the point on Earth's surface above the focus. The most damage is usually near the epicenter. Energy from an earthquake moves in waves.

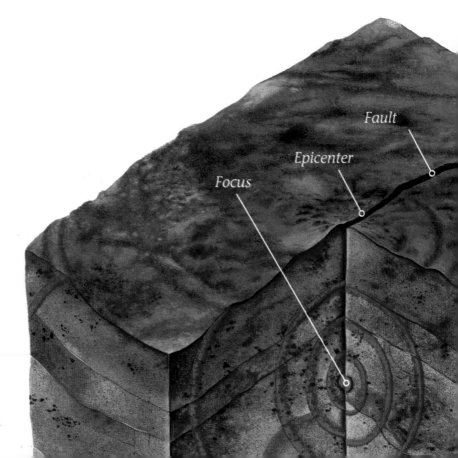

Fault

Epicenter

Focus

Effects of Earthquakes and Volcanoes

Many places on Earth have earthquakes and volcanoes. In 1815 Mount Tambora in Asia erupted. Ash darkened the sky. Less sunlight reached Earth. This caused snow to fall in the northeastern United States in June.

In 1883 Krakatoa erupted in Indonesia. This volcano caused huge waves called tsunamis in Earth's oceans. Earthquakes can also cause tsunamis. Tsunamis can lead to landslides.

Two plates meet in California along the San Andreas Fault. Many earthquakes happen along this fault. Most are small. Some are very powerful.

Weathering, erosion, and deposition change Earth's landforms. So do landslides, earthquakes, and volcanoes. Earth's surface will always be changing.

Earthquakes can cause great damage.

Glossary

deposition   the laying down of pieces of Earth's surface after erosion

earthquake   the sudden movement of plates that makes Earth's crust shake

epicenter   the point on Earth's surface above the spot where plates start to move

erosion   the process of moving weathered rock

fault   a break or crack in rocks where Earth's crust can move

landform   a shape or natural feature found on Earth's surface

landslide   the quick downhill movement of great amounts of rock and soil

volcano   a landform with an opening out of which lava pours from below Earth's crust

weathering   the physical or chemical process by which rocks slowly break into smaller pieces